A **W**EDDING BOOK

PRINTED IN SINGAPORE

ISBN: 0-8118-2741-0

EDITED AND DESIGNED BY TOM MORGAN, BLUE DESIGN

10 9 8 7 6 5 4 3 2 1

CHRONICLE BOOKS
85 SECOND STREET
SAN FRANCISCO, CA 94105
WWW.CHRONICLEBOOKS.COM

A WEDDING BOOK

PHOTOGRAPHY BY DEBORAH SCHENCK

CHRONICLE BOOKS

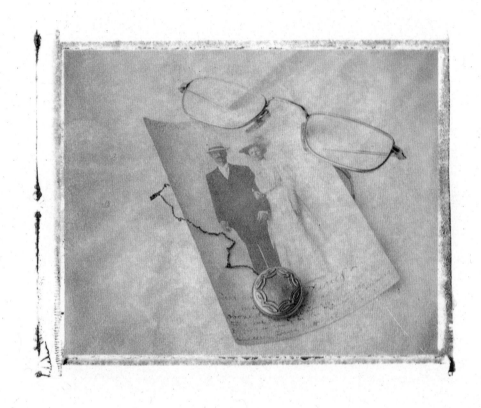

THE *B* ETROTHAL

We Get Engaged

ENGAGEMENT MEMENTO

DATE: _____

LOCATION: _____

_____

HOW IT HAPPENED: _____

_____

_____

_____

_____

WEDDING DATE:

_____

BRIDE'S SIGNATURE:

_____

GROOM'S SIGNATURE:

_____

MEMENTO

Our Engagement Party

HOSTED BY: _____

DATE: _____

LOCATION: _____

_____

_____

MEMENTO

$\mathcal{B}$RIDESMAIDS

_____

_____

_____

_____

_____

_____

_____

_____

NAME: _____

ADDRESS: _____

_____

(PHOTO)

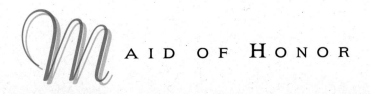

MAID OF HONOR

GROOMSMEN

_____

_____

_____

_____

_____

_____

_____

_____

_____

NAME: _____

ADDRESS: _____

_____

(PHOTO)

BRIDAL SHOWER

INVITATION (PASTE HERE)

HOSTED BY: _____

LOCATION: _____

_____

_____

GUEST LIST

_____

_____

_____

_____

_____

_____

_____

_____

_____

BRIDAL SHOWER PHOTO

GIFT WRAP SWATCHES AND RIBBONS

BRIDAL SHOWER GIFTS

GIFT: FROM:

GIFT: FROM:

GIFT: FROM:

GIFT: FROM:

GIFT: FROM:

GIFT: FROM:

GIFT: FROM:

GIFT: FROM:

GIFT: FROM:

GIFT: FROM:

GIFT: FROM:

GIFT: FROM:

BACHELOR PARTY

MEMENTOS (COCKTAIL NAPKIN, CIGAR-BAND, ETC.)

LOCATION: _____

_____

_____

_____

GUEST LIST

_____

_____

_____

_____

_____

_____

_____

_____

_____

_____

THE ARRANGEMENTS

(PASTE HERE)

CEREMONY

PHOTO

NAME: _____

PROCESSIONAL MUSIC: _____

RECESSIONAL MUSIC: _____

READERS: _____

READINGS: _____

VOCALISTS: _____

SONGS: _____

_____

_____

_____

_____

_____

_____

_____

_____

_____

_____

$\mathscr{R}$ E C E P T I O N

LOCATION: _____

_____

_____

COLOR SCHEME: _____

_____

_____

_____

_____

_____

PHOTOGRAPHER: _____

VIDEOGRAPHER: _____

REHEARSAL DINNER TOASTS

_____

_____

_____

_____

_____

_____

_____

_____

_____

_____

_____

REHEARSAL AND REHEARSAL DINNER

SIGNING THE LICENSE

(PHOTO HERE)

DINNER LOCATION: _____

_____

MENU: _____

_____

_____

_____

_____

_____

_____

_____

_____

_____

_____

_____

_____

_____

_____

$\mathcal{W}$EDDING ATTIRE

BRIDAL GOWN AND VEIL DESCRIPTION: _____

_____

_____

FABRIC SAMPLES

SOMETHING OLD: _____

SOMETHING NEW: _____

SOMETHING BORROWED: _____

SOMETHING BLUE: _____

ENGRAVED ON THE RINGS: _____

_____

BRIDAL BOUQUET AND BRIDESMAIDS' BOUQUETS (LIST FLOWERS USED): _____

_____

_____

BOUTONNIERE (LIST FLOWERS USED): _____/_____

_____

(PHOTO HERE)

FABRIC SAMPLES

(PHOTO HERE)

NAME: _____

FATHER OF THE BRIDE

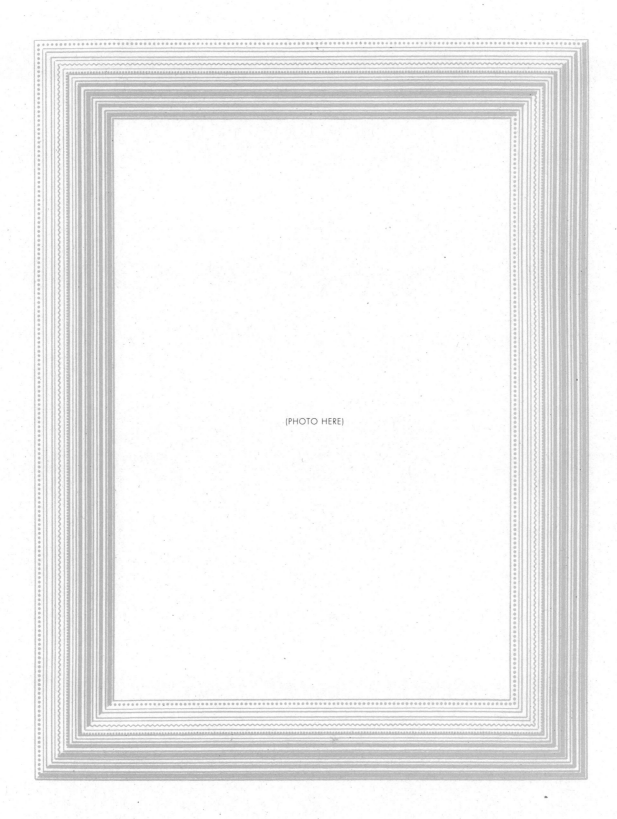

(PHOTO HERE)

NAME: _____

(PHOTO HERE)

NAME: _____

(PHOTO HERE)

NAME: _____

CONGRATULATIONS FROM FAMILY & FRIENDS

THE DAY

PREPARING FOR THE CEREMONY

THE BRIDE DESCRIBES HER DAY:

_____

_____

_____

_____

_____

_____

_____

_____

_____

THE GROOM DESCRIBES HIS DAY:

LAST MINUTE JITTERS

GROOM'S DESCRIPTION:

_____

_____

_____

_____

_____

BRIDE'S DESCRIPTION:

_____

_____

_____

_____

_____

(NEWSPAPER CLIPPING)

OFFICIANT

NAME: _____

(PHOTO)

 ows

_____

_____

_____

_____

_____

_____

_____

_____

_____

_____

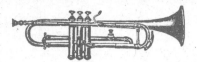

THE B AND

NAME: _____

BAND PLAY LIST:

_____

_____

_____

_____

_____

_____

_____

_____

_____

PRESS OF WEDDING FLOWERS

SONG TITLE: _____

LYRICS: _____

_____

_____

_____

_____

_____

_____

_____

(PHOTO HERE)

DESCRIPTION: _____

_____

_____

_____

_____

_____

_____

_____

(PHOTO HERE)

BEST MAN'S TOAST

(PHOTO HERE)

TOAST: _____

_____

_____

_____

GIFTS

GIFT: _____ FROM: _____

GIFT: _____ FROM: _____

GIFT: _____ FROM: _____

GIFT: _____ FROM: _____

GIFT: _____ FROM: _____

GIFT: _____ FROM: _____

GIFT: _____ FROM: _____

GIFT: _____ FROM: _____

GIFT: _____ FROM: _____

GIFT: _____ FROM: _____

GIFT: _____ FROM: _____

GIFT: _____ FROM: _____

GIFT: _____ FROM: _____

GIFT: _____ FROM: _____

GIFT: _____ FROM: _____

GIFT: _____ FROM: _____

GIFT: _____ FROM: _____

GIFT: _____ FROM: _____

GIFT: _____ FROM: _____

GIFT: _____ FROM: _____

GIFT: _____ FROM: _____

GIFT: _____ FROM: _____

GIFT: _____ FROM: _____

GIFT: _____ FROM: _____

GIFT: _____ FROM: _____

GIFT: _____ FROM: _____

GIFT: _____   FROM: _____

GIFT: _____   FROM: _____

GIFT: _____   FROM: _____

GIFT: _____   FROM: _____

GIFT: _____   FROM: _____

GIFT: _____   FROM: _____

GIFT: _____   FROM: _____

GIFT: _____   FROM: _____

GIFT: _____   FROM: _____

GIFT: _____   FROM: _____

GIFT: _____   FROM: _____

GIFT: _____   FROM: _____

GIFT: _____   FROM: _____

GIFT: _____ FROM: _____

GIFT: _____ FROM: _____

GIFT: _____ FROM: _____

GIFT: _____ FROM: _____

GIFT: _____ FROM: _____

GIFT: _____ FROM: _____

GIFT: _____ FROM: _____

GIFT: _____ FROM: _____

GIFT: _____ FROM: _____

GIFT: _____ FROM: _____

GIFT: _____ FROM: _____

GIFT: _____ FROM: _____

GIFT: _____ FROM: _____

GIFT: _____ FROM: _____

GIFT: _____ FROM: _____

GIFT: _____ FROM: _____

GIFT: _____ FROM: _____

GIFT: _____ FROM: _____

GIFT: _____ FROM: _____

GIFT: _____ FROM: _____

GIFT: _____ FROM: _____

GIFT: _____ FROM: _____

GIFT: _____ FROM: _____

GIFT: _____ FROM: _____

GIFT: _____ FROM: _____

GIFT: _____ FROM: _____

GIFT: _____ FROM: _____

GIFT: _____ FROM: _____

GIFT: _____ FROM: _____

GIFT: _____ FROM: _____

GIFT: _____ FROM: _____

GIFT: _____ FROM: _____

GIFT: _____ FROM: _____

GIFT: _____ FROM: _____

GIFT: _____ FROM: _____

GIFT: _____ FROM: _____

GIFT: _____ FROM: _____

GIFT: _____ FROM: _____

GIFT: _____ FROM: _____

GIFT: _____ FROM: _____

GIFT: _____ FROM: _____

GIFT: _____ FROM: _____

GIFT: _____ FROM: _____

GIFT: _____ FROM: _____

GIFT: _____ FROM: _____

GIFT: _____ FROM: _____

GIFT: _____ FROM: _____

GIFT: _____ FROM: _____

GIFT: _____ FROM: _____

GIFT: _____ FROM: _____

GIFT: _____ FROM: _____

GIFT: _____ FROM: _____

GIFT: _____ FROM: _____

GIFT: _____ FROM: _____

GIFT: _____ FROM: _____

(NAPKINS, MATCHBOOK, WINE LABEL, ETC.)

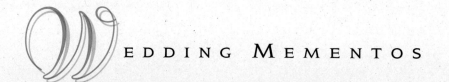

WEDDING MEMENTOS

(PHOTO HERE)

TRANSPORTATION: _____

_____

THE *H*ONEYMOON

TICKET STUBS

ITINERARY

_____

_____

_____

_____

_____

_____

_____

_____

_____

FIRST NIGHT ACCOMMODATIONS

(POSTCARD HERE)

HOTEL NAME: _____

ADDRESS: _____

HONEYMOON VIEW

(PHOTO HERE)

LOCATION: _____

DATE: _____

WEDDING ANNOUNCEMENT

Marriage Certificate

THE THRESHOLD

(PHOTO HERE)

ADDRESS: _____

_____

_____